ANCHOR BOOKS

POETS FROM

THE MIDLANDS

First published in Great Britain in 1995 by
ANCHOR BOOKS
1-2 Wainman Road, Woodston,
Peterborough, PE2 7BU

SB ISBN 1 85930 096 0

Foreword

Anchor Books is a small press, established in 1992, with the aim of promoting readable poetry to as wide an audience as possible.

We hope to establish an outlet for writers of poetry who may have struggled to see their work in print.

The poems presented here have been selected from many entries. Editing proved to be a difficult and daunting task and as the Editor, the final selection was mine.

The poems chosen represent a cross-section of styles and content. They have been sent from all over the world, written by young and old alike, united in the passion for writing poetry.

I trust this selection will delight and please the authors and all those who enjoy reading poetry.

Andrew Head
Editor

CONTENTS

WANDERING

I watched a paper bag
  Blowing along the street
Skipping, hopping, dancing,
  Moving on winged feet
It clung on to the railings
  Watching people in West Park
No longer sad and lonely
  On a shelf, remote and dark
Which way shall I blow?
  Towards the school of proud St Judes
Past the old Steam Laundry
  Where terraced houses stood
Supermarkets then unheard of
  George Mason's reigned supreme
Ration books all signed and dated
  Had homes in Whitmore Reans
Trolley buses running
  They'd surely never end
Poles came off the wires
  In Court Road, just on the bend
Courtaulds in its glory
  Producing Celanese
Recall the old glue factory
  Phew it made me sneeze
The little paper bag
  Made its way to Leicester Square
Thinking, hoping, dreaming,
  Is the Penny Bazaar still there?
Like this scrap of paper
  I drift along in memory
Until my daughter whispers 'love you'
  With flowers from Jim Petrie

Y Greenway

THE ANSWERING SEA

'Backwood look!' To the break sea mounting
A white crest poised
               for a spawning shore
An up swell thrust
               of a red sail flaunting
And the sea birds reel
               from a wind chaffed sward

So salute the dawn
               though the sky gives warning
A target stretched
               and the luck that flows
With the prow set straight
               through the crystal morning
And a glimpse of a cove
               through the darkness grows

To take the chance
               what the day is bringing
The dreams that linger
               and the trust will grow
Take heart the day sees
               the spirits singing
The faith will stay
               and the doubts will go

Bernard Brunner

THE BLACK COUNTRY DIRGE

The colour has not changed, only its location.
It used to be a colour associated with factories and furnaces
But now it's more confined to faces.
People have come here to improve their lives,
In the factories, that have gone away,
The furnace sun has set in many a town.
Those who brought the African and Asian sun,
Now with white make dole queues longer run.
Where thriving industry long had stood,
Stands youth around to do no good.
Where the workshop of the world was to be found,
Drugs and prostitution now abound.
Disenchanted youth that's on the dole,
Manufacturing Cinderella in her role.
O the empty faces they are here,
Smoking drugs and drinking beer.
Youth is waiting on the dole,
For a Government with soul,
The blackcountry may never be forgotten,
But much of it lies dead and rotten.

B Morgan

WATERWAYS

Gliding through the waters dark
With elegance and ease,
Now mobile homes with bright decor
In yellows, reds and greens;
Each holds intricate tales from old
Of many battles fought,
As main transportation they became
From the factory to the port.

Through the harsh winds battling on
The noble horse would tow,
Coal and iron from the black country
With horses strength would flow.
Legging through the tunnels dark
Through icy waters green,
Down the cut to Tipton
Where furnaces did gleam.

Working heavy lock gates
Repeated time again,
Leading horses many miles
Walked strong, but weary men,
For everlasting days did seem
No hope of rest or sleep,
Teasing pubs along the way
But timing they must keep.

Towering factory chimneys
Blackened from the smoke,
Cast shades of grey for miles around
As furnaces are stoked.
Cargo loading, squealing rats,
Loud bangs as boats collide,
Muddy banks with nettles thick
Where cargo boats werc tied.

Remaining are the barges now
With comfort, style and speed;
Muddy banks hold natural life
For the wild to live and feed.
Inns and pubs along the way
Inviting, clean and bright,
Black country beauty to this day
From a once industrious sight.

Sara Russell

CONNOTATIONS IN A CONURBATION

Connotations in a conurbation
Are few and far between
Schools dole out factory fodder
And GCSEs for the keen.

Cracked paving stones are
Adorned with dog shit -
Careful stamping ground
For cogs that don't fit.

The child with nothing
But sex and sport
To anaesthetise
The next appearance in court.

And middle-aged teachers
Answer lonely hearts
In the Guardian,
As they too play their parts.

They churn not turn.
They answer not question.
Serve each other well
As we commune in Hell.

Jayson Burns

A WEST MIDLAND CITY

Sombre suited business men, surrounded by potted palms,
scurried from the bowels of glassed motels; tattered
documents in their arms.

A swathe of multi culture embraces the city wide.
Neath globuled fountains saried Indian ladies glide.

As pearls from oyster shells boutiques spill out their wares
on cool cobbled walkways with diminutive airs.
Each side of garish hoardings fast food outlets abound
Balti, Greek and Chinois aromas astound.

There's no sunrise or sunset in city array.
Just a plethora of commerce or culture palaces;
stealing distant horizons away.

Dorothy Kempson Jones

MOOR ST. 12:18

Pacing the low, dry light
on the midday station's shafts of stampy tarmac.

Dust and bits of leaf
eddy in the corner, sheltered
and spiralling the breeze sighs and settles
the air
sinks
in thick layers over the silent bodies
placed like chess pieces
to glance through the dream of themselves,
taken out of time to drift
forever, held like dolls on
platform 2.

Strange to think that, soon
a train will come
into the still-frame.

Rose Beauchamp

THE BRUMMIE ACCENT

And so what's wrong with the Brummie accent?
You lot seem to think you're all clever out there,
Just come to live or work in this city,
And you'll soon understand why we don't give a care.

We're smart, we Brummies, we're smart and we're free,
We only breathe air, the type we can see,
And if we feel like a swim we just go to a pool,
No dirty sea water, it's you that's the fool.

And what about shopping? We're really good at that,
We go to the markets but we don't purchase tat,
We go to The Row or The Rag or Bull Ring,
You can't come to Birmingham and not spend a thing.

Art galleries, museums, we're very proud of those,
So if you want culture just follow your nose,
To the centre of Brum where there are flowers and trees,
Does it amaze you that Brummies grew these?

It should not amaze you and you shouldn't bear a grudge,
Against a person's accent because you're no judge,
Just take the time to peep inside,
And you'll see why we Brummies wear our accents with pride.

Angela McNab

SOUL'S RELEASE

From the dark of a twisted tree,
A winged stranger called to me
And like a fool, I went to him -
Death's carrion cherubim.

But when he sang of his timeless song,
I found my fear to be woefully wrong
For he released my soul and set me free
With the peaceful power of his magic melody.

Mark Bane

WEST MIDLAND OUR PLACE

Here in the West Midlands we are very proud
We have got a great place, come and look around
There are many shops here, lots of different kind
Theatres too, and night clubs, places to unwind.
When in the city centre, shopping is a breeze
And when you're feeling worn out, you can take your ease.
There are all sorts of restaurants, cafe they abound
Lots and lots of buses to get you all around
Pictures you've been keeping, lurking in your mind
May not be the same one's as those you come and find
We look to the future, that is where we aim
Our past is still our heritage, but there is much to gain
If it's greener pastures you are looking for
Then you need look no further it's right here at our door
There's trees and fields, parks and lakes
We have got everything it takes.
There maybe other places for you to go and see
But the West Midlands, is the place to be.

I Taylor

THE CARNIVAL

Bright and colourful decked with pride
Happy feet trotting side by side
Holding the buckets that jingled aloud
Catching the offerings from the crowd.

So were the floats that passed our way
Through the town on carnival day
Spirits were high, the weather great
And lasting all day until it was late.

Pipe bands, bugle bands, classic and jazz
Music that helped the razzmatazz
Gay coloured dresses worn by the lasses
Brightened the scene with each float that passes.

All for a good cause was every event
Every penny was money well spent
Some went on stalls, handing out fishes
Some just got spent smashing up dishes

As the day started so did it end
Bright happy faces homeward to wend
Helped by the fact the weather kept fine
And all who attended had a rare time

Is all the work justified, all efforts made?
Especially all who worked so hard unpaid
Surely it was, a day to remember
If only creating the memories made.

Sam Izzard

PULLING UP ROOTS

The light of day
Startles my eyes
Knocking them sideways
The day I have both feared
And wanted has come.
I am to move from my
Cotton wool boundaries
To the sharp exterior
Of the world.
There is no guiding hand
No answer to the tasks I face,
Just me and my rucksack
And the arms of wilderness beckoning.

Sarah Paliukenas

PROGRESS

The factory floor falls silent.
It's Friday night once more.
This one is very different from
All the ones before.
For this is the final Friday
The one the workers dread.
No more that Monday
feeling the factory is dead.
Machines now lying silent
The last lights turned off.
The workers say their last
goodbyes, tears welling in their
eyes, as they recall a lifetime
spent inside those walls
Workers honest, loyal and true
What are they now supposed to do!

B R B George

DOLPHINS

You go and catch them and they die;
But all that we can do is cry,
We are not the only things
On earth who have families,
They do too,
So please stop it.

Dolphins, dolphins, dolphins,
Left to live or die,
Fishermen say that they don't catch them,
But we know that they lie,
So save the dolphins,
Yes save the dolphins,
So they can live not die.

Michael Rich (13)

RURAL SUBURB

It's a beautiful dawn in Moseley,
here in B13,
thrush and blackbird competing,
the garden's a glorious scene.

The fox has drunk at the bird bath.
The hedgehog has scuttled away.
I treasure this shy little creature
who's rarely seen by day.

The bluebells are back with a vengeance,
flushing the garden blue.
A few of the white and pink ones
say: 'Notice! *We're* here too!'

Squirrels chase in the oak tree
above the blue-tit's box,
wood-pigeons strut their stately way;
I hope they'll look out for the fox!

Now I've just seen a magpie
(I do so hope there'll be two!)
He's beautiful - like the dandelion,
and I don't want either, it's true.

But it's lovely to have all this beauty
with a busy city near.
We're really truly rural
in my Mosely garden here.

Geraldine Squires

UNTITLED

The years have passed and I have never forgot
your beautiful face I've treasured a lot.
I never thought I would ever see it again
But when I did my heart started to beat
again once more

Now the darkness has gone
The light shineth on
For the bad times have just begun (come)
What was done was done
Now, let's live for the future
and care for one another
I can only pray
We will sort things out one day

M B M

NO MILK TODAY!

Our milkman sells potatoes,
Ginger-beer and cokes.
He sells butter, cheese and bread-rolls
And eggs with double yolks.

He has oven-ready turkeys,
Mince-pies, fruit, ice-lollies.
Smoked and streaky bacon,
Carrots, peas and caulies.

All sorts of fruity yoghurts.
A dozen different cakes.
Orange squash and lemonade,
And buns like granny makes.

Christmas puds and cat-food
And cream as smooth as silk.
With so many goodies on his cart -

There's no room for our milk!

David Whitehead

MONDAY MORNING

Good morning Mrs Patterson, what was that you said?
And why is Sammy crying? Oh, the hamster's dead
Of course I'll keep an eye on him, he must be quite upset
Though it will be a good experience if he wants to be a vet.

Carefully Samantha Green, you've knocked poor Emma down
I know you didn't mean it dear, you needn't give a frown
Take those gloves off Richard Walsh, we don't wear those in class
And it's nice to say *excuse me* if you only want to pass.

Come on Jill and Valerie, it's time to come inside
And close the door behind you, you've left it open wide
I want to call the register, it's nearly ten past nine
Oh what's the matter Dipesh, do you really have to whine?

Is Samina Parmar here, I haven't seen her yet.
Stop stroking Linda's hair Shameen, you know she's not a pet.
Now where has David Thomas gone, I saw him by the gate
No you cannot be excused, Denise, you'll really have to wait.

Reading books out children please, just a page or two
While I'm sorting out the money for the trip to Twycross Zoo,
Yes, Zaheer, you've read your book, you told me that last week,
Whatever is Samira doing - playing hide and seek?

Ah, good evening Tony Anderson, I'm glad to see you're here
Slept in late again I see, the second time this year.
Oh dear me, whatever next, is Robert Parker yawning?
I can't believe you're tired yet, it's only Monday morning!

Catherine Mansell

FOR SARHA

Sarha was my loyal friend
I loved with all my heart
She was so beautiful right from the start
She was only a mongrel
A Heinz 57 they say
We had her for fourteen years
And treasured every day
She was just like my little girl
I loved in every way
She followed me everywhere
Even when I told her to stay
When she became poorly
I knew what I must do
I couldn't see her suffer
And I think she really knew
When she was put to sleep
I thought that I would die
But now I know she's resting
In heaven in the sky
I'll never forget you sweetheart
Although we are apart
For when you died
You took with you
A piece of my heart

Ann Smith

DAYDREAMS

A country pub, close to the sea,
That's what I would like for me.
Old stone floors, and timbered ceilings.
Brasses in the firelight gleaming.

Low dormer windows, facing the sea -
That would be the place for me.
Lying in a feathered bed -
A place to rest my weary head.

Listening to the quiet sea sighing,
And overhead the seagulls crying.
All this in my dreams I see -
Yes! That would be the place for me.

H Bailey

THE CANAL BOAT THEME

Decaying stones above the water
Shine clear like crystal mortar.
The stilling silence of the Sunday,
Reflect the mood for the solemn Monday.
The hazy dawn brings the sun -
As if, the world has just begun.
Autumn leaves rest on the ground -
Put there naturally without a sound.
The kingfisher hungry hunts the meal.
Breakfast is served to the church bell peal.

Later, onwards through the morn
Ripples of water wash the dawn.
Wildlife looms coloured and wintered,
Short days plan their lives so splintered.
Midday is here shrouded in the cold,
As the sky and trees soundly hold;
The wintry scene ready for snow.
The water's passage through the places;
Shows the people have seasoned faces.

Passing the waterside house of mirth,
Built on aged created earth,
Inside, men invite the joy
Dreaming the week's toil and ploy.
Drunken dreams shall not fail;
Prevailed and sounded by chilling ale.
Downwards, further toward a lock,
Where the boats of freedom dock;
Walk the lovers hand in hand
Over the *generations* peaceful land.

Eventide brings a soundless still,
Darkness falls o'er the land to fill,
Every corner of vision with the night,
So peaceful is the glowing light.
The light that shone before the morn,
Keeping the blessed strong and warm,
Cultured dreams explore the heart,
The world will never fall apart,
Upon a star rests tomorrow's dream,
See and feel *the canal boat theme*.

Andrew M Allington

THE LEAVES

Golden leaves that in the Autumn sunlight shine.
awaiting a wind that will force them to release their hold
from trees that have held them whether it be rain or fine
but now must face the winter upon ground that is cold.

When on the trees beneath a summer sky
leaves are admired by good folk passing by
but at last comes the time when they must fall
to be walked upon with no attraction at all
indeed they are a nuisance those same folk say
forgetting the visual joy that in the recent past they have provided
no longer the attractive shimmering display
as they are blown hither and thither with summer season subsided.

Come next spring and their successors will once again adorn those
same branches.
Covering the bareness created by the winter season
various green and other colours which springtime sunshine enhances
Inviting upwards glances if for no particular reason
other than to be thankful for nature's artistry in full bloom
to perhaps be remembered as we sweep up dead leaves with a broom.

Den Biggs

WEST MIDLANDS

Will you look with me to a hearty county,
Established by its memorable past,
Scenes of factories blackened and stoutly,
They break the skyline with shadows cast.

May I remind you how wealth was made,
In furnace and foundry,
Diligence, pride, a foundation laid,
Land that astounds me.
Ambitious people with hearts of gold,
Narrow boats, gypsies and farmers who tend,
Dwelling in a land so bold,
See here is West Midlands, my friend.

Wendy Hobbins

BELLIGERENT BLACKCOUNTRY

Cut against a backcloth of grime,
Some smoky silhouette of pain;
Long suffering Blackcountry.
Bruised, battered, but not beaten,
This resilient Music Hall joke.
Thrown away, cursed and avoided
Used and abused like a poor relative's inheritance.
The sore thumb with a heart of gold,
A speech impediment sitting on the motorway.
The belligerent Blackcountry.
Layers of landscaped dirt and dust.
You were not a pretty wench but you gave them all
so much more than they ever deserved.

Doug Parker

RIVER REA

Enclosed in concrete
Like nuclear waste.
Once proud and free,
Crowned with oak and thorn
Sacrificed for the good of men.
You lie entombed
Waiting to rise again
To throw off these chains
And proclaim freedom to captives.
Waiting to rise again
To break down the walls
And pour forth, a highway of living water.
Waiting to rise again
To renew life
And bequeath natural chaos to a blinkered nation.

David Massey

AS WE SUPPLY THE PRAYER
(Dedicated to Tom and Doris Julien)

Down on our knees
Yet up in the heavenlies
Bringing hearts before His throne
We intercede for some broken heart
Who'll find life in Him alone

Prayer touches the heart of God
It's moving the hand
That can heal them
Prayers touching the heart of God
Their life He'll provide, He'll provide
As we supply the prayers

What is the price?
Is it too much to pay?
To save one precious life
If we sow in tears,
We shall reap with joy.
He who wins a soul is wise.

A tear touches the heart of God
It's moving the hand
That can save them
Tears touching the heart of God
Their life He'll provide, He'll provide
As we supply the tears

Down come the walls
As He draws men to Himself.
We see the miracle that's wrought
Pray for the labourers
He'll send them to His harvest
He'll provide them all, He'll provide
As we supply the prayers

David Schwan

TOUCH TYPING

A young girl
Sitting at a typewriter.
Her tight skirt
Creased into deliberate folds.
Sitting upright
Tightlipped.
Eyes
Staring straight ahead at the white wall.
Fingers
Prodding wilfully at the black keys.

Patricia Bullock

NOVEMBER 1993

A sprinkling of snow covers the ground
All is quiet - not a soul around
A peek through the curtains shows it's still dark
There's definitely no-one playing in the park
We creep downstairs as quiet as a mouse
Mustn't wake anyone else in the house
We open the door and dash for the toys
I play along like one of the boys
Race the cars along the tracks
Play rough and tumble and roll on our backs
Push the trucks along the floor
Until they crash into the door
Next we'll read the books and when we're done
We will have had such a lot of fun
I don't mind playing games but please tell me
Why, son, do your days have to start so early
It's only five thirty!

D Lineker

TIME

I was walking through life.
I felt as I always remembered feeling,
The trees grew as they had always grown,
Around me the sun shone and the birds sang.
Everything was familiar.
Once, I remember,
I looked behind me
And saw a speck in the distance,
Moving at my pace.
Each time I looked it was there,
Millions of miles away,
Until I stopped looking.
I was walking through life.
The trees grew as they had always grown,
The sun shone and the birds sang,
But everything was not familiar.
I turned.
A huge shadow bent over me,
Passed through me,
Overtook me.
There on the horizon
As I sank down
I saw a figure, glancing back,
Casual.
It could see
A speck in the distance,
But time had overtaken me.

Ruth Calder

PENN COMMON

The common is a beautiful place,
Lots and lots of open space,
To walk and look and gaze around,
At wonders growing from the ground.

Different types of flowers, colours bright and new,
Just sitting there growing specially for you.
Trees of every shade and size, clouds above their tops
Meadows in the distance, throwing forth their crops.

Butterflies dancing all around,
Then sitting on the flowers,
Just go, look and take it in,
For hours and hours and hours.

Les Hinton

UNFULFILLED AMBITION

That unfulfilled ambition
Surrendered now to time,
Seemed burdened by condition
Impossible to climb,
And yet it was not so
And worst of all you know!

J Summerfield

BIRMINGHAM

Dear Birmingham, you're home to me,
You'll always be first, not the second city,
From big Brum's chimes, to your dusty streets,
You're mine from winter's cold to summer's heats.

The Rotunda, the landmark that cleaves the sky,
Will always be first to catch the visitor's eye,
The Bull ring markets, fruit, flowers, crockery,
Pet stores, toys and haberdashery.

St Martins-in-the-Bull-Ring, whose lofty spire
Keeps a loving watch over the sweet-voiced choir,
The rag-market, the row market, fashions galore,
You'll find anything you want at a market stall.

The pavilions and the palisades, many stores
Tier on tier, on numerous floors;
The hub of the city - offices and banks
Spread out to join factories in dingy ranks.

Canal barges ply their way,
A mode of transport of yesterday:
Diamond merchants, jewellers, traders in gold,
The jewellery quarter still maintains a foothold.

The science museum, the art gallery,
Theatres and night-clubs, the Hall of Memory,
The ring roads, the carriageways decked with flowers,
Come to Birmingham - I promise you many happy hours!

M J de'Vandre

I WAS BEAUTIFUL ONCE . . .

She stands there, before
The mirror.
Staring at a beautiful face
That could be better.

Then she begins.
The operation,
The overhaul,
The transformation.

From something
Beautiful
To something better.

To be, someone special
Someone they'll lust after.
And when she's gone
Remember forever.

Karen Miller

HOMING PIGEONS

Rennes,
  Lamballe,
    Bordeaux!
      Sebastian,
        Santander,
          Pau!

Stretching their skill to the limit
As further and further they go.

Whirl of white wings
'Gainst the dark of the storm,
Clap of white wings,
Pale grey skimmings
Close to the fancier's head,
A cool disturbance of air on his cheek,
Herald a landing straight as a die!
Blunt peck of beak on the palm of his hand,
Throaty-croaky *Curr-roo! Curr-roo! Curr-roo!*
Says,
They're home!

Eileen Turner

UNTITLED

Wait till I've recovered my breath,
Till the remnants
Of fears almighty cascade
Have trickled away
And are lost.
Delay your approach
Till the final hour
Of the darkest night,
When serenity
Has played a part
In sending me to sleep.
And only then,
Come silently,
With stifled steps
And show me
That brighter road
On which you journeyed to me.
And at its end
We'll awake to our world,
And the idyll of our minds
May be realised.
And we shall share,
The coldest years of our lives,
Undisturbed by the storms
Of our frightened past.

Alison Hope

DOUBLE TAKE

Tall and slim. Muscles taut.
Leaning backwards. Left foot forward,
Right arm rearward. Knees and ankles
Slightly bent. Javelin pointing
To the sky. Such a statue.
Such a stillness. Movement captured.

Thrower ready, rearward stretches.
Muscles tighter. Fingers clenched.
Lurches forward, hurling javelin.
Javelin arching through the air.
Sailing upwards. Rushing smoothly.
Downward pointing. Landing quietly.

Morning paper shows the thrower
Leaping upwards, punching air.
Exultation! Calls this picture:
Javelin thrower - movement captured!

Juanita Watson

UNTITLED

I sit here looking outside
the weather's really great
I look at my watch
and think he's running late;
he takes me for granted
he knows that I will wait
but one of these fine days
he'll find that it's too late
I start to get up from my chair
the tears flow from my eyes
I've waited just a little too long
we now must say goodbye

Elaine Franks

A SUMMER'S DAY (IN A SUBURBAN GARDEN)

Among the trees
Ruffled by the breeze
Red-topped houses stand.
The sun shines, white
Through wisp-clouds, bright
On the flickering, countless leaves.

The laburnum offers its gifts
Of beauty as it spreads
The golden chains in drifts
Lovingly hung on delicate threads.

The purple-thimbled foxglove
Is o'er seen from above
By the rose-crowned bower
That sweetens the passing hour.

Glowing peonies, red
Gently nod their globed heads.
Stately lavenders congregate
Recalling refined tales of yesterdate.

Where once the lovely lilacs gleamed
There are now dead clusters of umber
A year will pass before is seen
Again the sweet-scented splendour.

J T Purdom

UNTITLED

I have a friend that I hold dear,
she's worth her weight in gold,
She's with me through both thick and thin,
her faith it goes untold.
She will offer me her shoulder
when things go sadly wrong,
If I feel down and helpless,
I know that she'll be strong.
She is a friend I can't replace,
she's a one of that's for sure,
she's there for me both night and day,
My troubles she'll endure,
I simply can't confuse her,
with anyone else I know,
When darkened clouds surround me,
her love she'll always show.
I'm speaking of one woman,
and not of any other,
Of whom I speak so highly?
Yes! You guessed! My dearest mother.

Linda Moore

PUBERTY ON A TRAIN (7.26 AM, BIRMINGHAM TO LONDON)

A little girl wearing a soft blue hat,
      Is sprinting forward while quietly sat;
Staring out with cool grey eyes,
      At rusted rails and passing lives.
A fair angel flying from her mother's lap,
      Into a mundane adult's trap.

Pretty girl, cling tight to your childish spirit,
      Do not give up your last innocent minute.
Puberty mourns a lost golden day,
      When a heart warmed baby learned to play.
Child step through a pasture green,
      Far from the dark-filled adolescent scream;
And be sure to take your maiden's grace,
      To wherever life's loves makes your place.

John Anderton

'DIVINE' HE SAID

Not too loud, just clear.
He spoke
Words of the Lord
Written in his heart.
Extreme attention
He rarely slips his sight.
I am his focus
He seeks for me.
Clumsy am I;
Shaking confidence.
Too crippled
To keep alert.
He laughs a little,
Touches philosophy.
Dreams of a
Good world - like me.
Music is the remedy
For morning blues.
I ask myself
To live and let live.
Spare the world
From my blues
As, he does for me.
Close enough
To make love
With words.
I ask of his health.
Hesitant? He is not
And tells me;
He feels *divine*.

Dex

43

MY POEM

Who has made this great big world,
Our dear Lord above,
The flowers, birds and everything
He made with all His love.
The oceans deep, the mountains
High, the sky so big and blue
Our dear Lord made all things,
Because His love is true,

S Jackson

PARTY DAY

The striped waves in which we live
Are turbulent on party day,
We have one arm and single action
To drink and keep despair away,
Legless, our dark yet merry crowd,
Floats and spins round and round
The huge black cauldron they surround.
The whites of our eyes and shallow ears
Heightened by the belly's magic beer:
Become overshadowed by inky abstination
Down, sink I. My fear and concernation
Drown. Drink the gloomy turbulation,
Of this grimy everlasting damnation.

Emma Daniel

TOM BOY MARY

There was a young girl called Mary
Who liked to dress up as a fairy
She had a big wand
Which she waved o'er the throng
Till she tripped and fell straight on her derri(ere)

She got a bit older
And some say much bolder
Oh heavens what will she do now
She bought roller skates
That her mother just hates
And whizzed down the mall shouting wow!

Her skates kept on going
With no way of knowing
When she would be able to stop
Till a boat trailer came past
With a yacht and big mast
And she ended up on the top

She got to her teens
And still liked climbing trees
She was better than boys of her age
But one day quite late
Alone with no mate
Zoo keepers put her in a cage

Now she's a young mother
And there's no more bother
Well at least that's what you'd think
But call any day
If it's not out of your way
She'll be standing on her head at the sink!

Mary McPhee

OUR TOWN

Ugly graffiti daubed
on walls
Our town has seen
better days.
Blackened chimneys dot
the landscape
shimmering in a
summer haze.
The factory girls
chat away idly,
waiting for the *shift*
to begin.
Whilst out in Suburbia
the upper classes
sip away at their lime
juice and gin.
Yet, beside the
canal, pretty wild flowers,
flourish and thrive in
the Smethwick air,
and the bustling streets seem
far away
as peace and tranquillity comes
to those there.

Margaret Maher

THE LITTLE TEAPOT

I went to a car boot
To see what I could buy
I wandered round the tables
When something caught my eye

There a little tea pot
With a crack across the lid
I ask the bloke how much it was
He said it's yours for just a quid

I knocked him down to 50p
Then happy as could be
Put it in the side board
With the other twenty three

I've always collected teapots
Since I was just a kid
Some with broken spouts
This one - a broken lid.

I don't like silly tea bags
Most people use today
I warm the pot then let it stand
The good old fashioned way

When my friend calls round
As fed up as can be
I say don't cry, sit down, my dear,
I'll make a pot of tea

Harry C Wragg

JUST PASSING THROUGH

Just passing through, I'm a stranger in town,
Just me, my camera and my walkman, the batteries run down,
I can't begin to express my feelings,
With people making dodgy dealings,
I feel like an outsider looking in,
A world that's alien and full of sin,
I seem to knock but no one answers,
So I carry on knocking waiting to come in,

Just passing through, I'm a stranger in town,
Banging my head against a brick wall,
Nothing means anything to me any more,
I ask a question and get no reply,
The English it seems don't want to try,
So once again I'm on my own,
In a strange country miles from home,

The city centre that's known as town,
Has lots of people from miles around,
Most speak English and some speak French,
I walk past a young man sleeping on a bench,
He is sleeping there for all to see,
A man that was once like you and me,
So the next time you go to town,
Don't be a stranger just passing through,
Take care of Birmingham and Birmingham will take care of you.

Amy Robertson

CITY SUMMERTIME LOVE

I stroll through the city park,
The sun streams through the emerald leaves,
I'm captive in my daydream world,
Summertime smiles down on me.

Pink blossom flutters to the ground,
A unique perceptual paradise,
And as I drowse the day away,
Tranquillity does this tide entice.

The cool fresh breeze blows through my heart,
Green grass below, blue skies above,
I hum myself a blissful tune,
I'm feeling free and deep in love.

My head's held high in the summer air,
Away from the hustle and bustle of town,
I sit by the stream and dream of my love,
I wonder what she's doing now.

At peace with my mind in the blazing sun,
Remembering all the happy times,
And even though we're miles apart,
Our hearts, our souls are forever entwined.

Tristan Harris

MALINGERER

O mother, please don't make me go,
I really am unwell,
I think I've caught Malaria
I'm sure that you can tell.

Or maybe I've got Leprosy
So I'll stay hidden in my room,
And if I have to go to school today,
You'll send me to by doom.

Now mother, please do listen,
It really isn't true,
That I've been crayoning Measles spots
And sticking them on with glue.

I know my brother Billy
Says that I'm telling you a tale
But just you look upon my face,
Don't you think that I look pale.

No, that isn't just a flour bag
That's underneath my bed.
It's really a cold poultice
I've been wearing on my head.

You'd better take my temperature
I'm feeling quite unsteady,
What do you mean its Sunday?
Gosh, I'm feeling better already!

Karen Smith

THE ROAD TO STAFFORD

Walk down the narrow, mile-long hill from Garshall Green,
There, in the valley, Milwich Village can then be seen.
Side by side, the mixture of homes old and new,
Clustered below the ancient church, comes into view.

Left at the Village Hall and right at The Green Man,
Pass the church; walk quickly up Cromer Bank, if you can!
Now down the lane with Lord Harroby's farms on
Either side, and soon you will arrive at Sandon.

Now cross the A51 with care and caution.
The road is busy, but there is a path to walk on.
At The Dog and Doublet pub you must turn right
And the old canal bridge will then come into sight.

Stop a while at Sandon Lock and lean on the wall,
Watch holiday makers at the lock gates, hear them call.
Walk on over the bridge and climb up the hill,
Rejoice that no increased mining leaves Salt there still.

Down the hill past Hopton's ancient battle site, tramp,
All around you can be seen Stafford RAF camp.
Now here is Beaconside, to be crossed with care,
Pass the industrial park and you're nearly there.

On past the houses, past Lotus Shoes on one side,
On past pub and chip shop, then the prison can be spied.
Walk past well defended doors and prison wall,
On to the roundabout and view the clock tower tall.

Look down the High Street, city shops on either side,
Behind, the ancient churches of Chad and Mary hide.
Up on the hill, the castle ruin looks down
And I'm by the Ancient High House in Stafford town.

Sheila E Harvey

WELCOME TO STOKE-ON-TRENT

We invite you to drive
around six towns not five,
You'll be in for a surprise
if you expect ash filled skies

Gone now are the bottle kilns
dusty and bleak,
No more caps that are flat
with peaks

People now go for walks
where the air is now clean,
Along country parks
in our fields of green.

We still produce china
it's the finest and best.
You won't find any finer
we far excel the rest.

So come one, come all,
stroll down our terraced streets.
See our market stalls and
the potteries shopping centre that
Stands so tall,
you'll be in for quite a treat.

Come shopping in our towns
it's a real pleasure.
You're bound to go home
with gifts to treasure.

Take a tour around Gladstone museum,
you'll be glad you went to see them,
With scenes from the past
take home memories that will last.

So if your life is dull
please, come pay us a call.

Phillip N Dawson

MORE QUESTIONS THAN ANSWERS

Staffordshire where is that they say
in the middle of somewhere
North West say the Potteries
West Midlands say the Black Country

How do they speak?
Brummie? No I am from Tamworth
Northern? No I am from Stoke
Derbyshire? No I am from Burton

What is there?
A big theme park
the Peak District not many know that
and plenty of space in the middle

What do they do?
They make beer Burtons gift to the world
nice china from Stoke
cattle markets in Uttoxeter
the Black Country? Well it's still there

Famous people?
Samuel Johnson inventor of the dictionary
Robert Plant of Led Zeppelin
Slade
and Robbie from Take That

Where is the focus?
We don't know.

James Moore

TO BE FREE

Where insanity reigns,
Down all the lanes.
And violence breeds.
Dogs off leads,
The attractive,
                    held captive,
By wedding rings.
and other things.

This is Stoke-on-Trent,
Bodies for rent,
But something is amiss,
The whole world,
                    is like this,

All we can hope,
Is one day our rope,
Will finally snap
Our bones will crack
Only then we'll be
                    finally free.

Lord Pondle

CLAY POTS

Oh these people of the pots,
See how they rise rough,
Out of the Staffordshire clay.

Voices raised in protest
Cry out against the changing day,
Once forced shaped,

Into bottom-knockers
and oat-cake eaters
such quaint vessels unbroken

Famous world-wide,
for the common dialect,
and awesome pottery,

The pass into obscurity,
no interest, no pay
Just a sad, stale society,

no longer able to make
its way
          into the firing kiln.

Ros Lee

AROUND THE GRAVE OF MOLLY LEIGH
(THE BURSLEM WITCH)

Around the grave of Molly Leigh
A strangely sight there is to see
For when the Bursley Bells toll twelve
There gathers goblins, sprites and elves;
There gathers imps and sour faced things
That demons of the darkness brings
And toads with snails and slugs and bats
Come to meet the graveyard cats.
A weird array of grotesque faces
That congregate from many places.
Hanley, Longton, Tunstall Sytch
They come to see the Burslem witch
And there upon her crumbling stone
They knock to see if she's at home.
They cry out loud, 'Oh Molly Leigh,
Chase us round the apple tree!'
But as every local ought to know
She only sends her talking crow.
The crow that hates mischievous fun
And swears and curses everyone.
For when the shadows start to creep
Molly's ghost remains asleep.
Around the grave of Molly Leigh
A strangely sight there is to see,
For when the Bursley bells toll one
Those goblins, sprites and elves are gone.

Vince Marsden

WINNOTH DALE

Not far from the towers with its mighty rides
Lies the hamlet in the dale, narrow lanes with high sides
Where the cockerel heralds morning as it echoes all around
And from the hills thereabouts comes hardly a sound.

But the notice on the chapel disappeared with age
And the sound of singing from every turned page
No longer can be heard, although the building still stands
And the welcome it once gave, has turned to other hands.

And the hamlet in the valley called Winnoth Dale
Where water springs forth, without fail
Is scattered with farms and houses too
And the horses with their owners in the morning pass thro!

Where Alton Towers has it thousands from every walk and climb
The dale still sleeps, as untouched by time
And the walkers on a Sunday, the fresh air to take
As the farmers on a week day a living have to make.

A J Plant

MY XMAS PRESENTS

A Stoke City shirt,
down past my knees.
Jockey shorts covered
in Santas, and bright Xmas trees.

A set of garden tools,
to keep me busy.
A small potted plant,
could be, a Busy Lizzie?

Blue coloured diary,
for the months ahead.
Complete with biro,
that's bright red.

A large photo album but,
without any mounts.
Still like they always say,
it's the thought that counts!

N Plant

WIRKSWORTH TO DERBY

The spectrum of greens have painted the countryside,
For everyone to see on this ride,
Wining roads between hills and pubs,
Golden autumn leaves falling onto woods,
A contrast from the big smoke,
Here they call people folk,
On my travels these strangers I meet,
Where they're always keen to greet,
I see an horizon of perfectly lined trees,
Underneath elegant deer walk with ease,
Ivy grows wild over a green mouldy wall,
I hear the sheep's call,
The blue water moves silently and slow,
While the fishermen line up in a row,
Next time could be different to what I've been shown,
But in my travels and observations I'll never be alone.

Alison Winfield

THE MILK HERD

'The heifers a 'bulling' I cried to my mate
Then as typical farmers we leaned on the gate
Whilst the man AI'd her with what's called a straw
All this of course costing money galore
Months later on she is examined by the vet
Expenses still rising no return for it yet
He will hopefully confirm that the heifers in calf
Then we feed her and bed her for near on nine months and a half
The cost is increasing as no doubt you now see
But still no idea what the sex is to be
Heifers are usually reared and run on
Until old enough to have a daughter or son
But a bull must be sold no space to be reared
A profit on him will never be cleared
He is taken to market and put through the auction
My cash flow improves the bank views with caution
The calf now moves on - near or far maybe
But a wonderful beginning he has had whilst with me
For this is the cycle of a cows life
To produce the milk for the countries housewife
Just nature that has been here since time first began
Change should not be made by woman or man
There is an alternative that would give us no mirth
Give us a subsidy to shoot bull calves at birth.

Connie Barker

DERBYSHIRE

Oh rolling hills of Derbyshire,
With dales all hues of green,
Your acreage so beautiful,
A peaceful, tranquil scene.

There's busy hives of industry
Aside the rivers clear,
Now clean and babbling as of old,
Delight to eye and ear.

The villages of natural stone,
Those Torrs topped with cloud,
This is my own Derbyshire,
A land of which I'm proud.

So heed these words and learn
Of places, views and bounty,
Everyone should come to see
Derbyshire, my home county.

Ade Hall

NOVEMBER BLEAKLOW SUMMIT

The rain, you expect. Rain
Flung into your face like shards of quartz
And a wind with claws to pull you down,
But the bare brown bleakness of the sullen moor
Stuns, like the Somme's devastation,
With its ferocious monotony.

At twenty yards a bleached sheep skull
Explodes into the sprint of a mountain hare.
Twitching, shell-shocked, his coat anticipating snow
He zig-zags to his trench, dodging bullets,
Awaiting the next storm salvo.

David Peggs

YOUR ABSENCE

(Written in Beeley for Norma,
Whose golden hair shines so bright
It can be seen without eyesight.)

The rhododendrons don
Robes of frost,
Each crow is concussed,
Each butterfly lost.
The stream had once reflected your hair,
It conjured from curls,
Tiaras and pearls.
Petals, like plectrums, plucked in the air.
Now the wind is worried,
Too worried to blow,
The stream too sorry to flow.
In your absence,
There stalls a hearse formed of cloud,
Storms and stomachs churn.
A breeze will burn and shrivel the shroud
When you, my love, return.
The marsupial spring
Will pull from its purse
Confetti, and sprinkle the hearse.
But now the wind is worried,
Much too weary to blow,
The spring too shy to show.

Rogan M Sutton

DERBYSHIRE

Our dream was always to retire
To the green open spaces of Derbyshire.
A tiny cottage nestling in the peak.
Our dream has now come true.
A home, though tiny, that has a view
Of rolling hills to front and rear.
In warm and sunny days
We take to the roads and by-ways,
To picnic by peaceful rivers and lakes,
Or visit some vast estate and stately home
Where pheasant, fox and red deer roam,
And indulge in tea and home-made cakes.
The *Alpine* beauties of Matlock Bath,
The healing waters of Buxton Spa,
Dove Dale and the limestone rock,
Tissington and the Dressing of Wells.
At Hayfield watch men run on the Fells,
Or sheep dogs rounding up their flock,
Or climb the dizzying heights of Kinder Scout.
Join the hikers, get out and about.
Perhaps stride on the Pennine Way.
In Castleton they have their Garland
With dancers, lord and lady and a marching band
To celebrate Royal Oak Day.
In Chesterfield they have a crooked spire.
At Parsley hey they have cycles for hire
To keep you fit whilst you explore.
And history here abounds
With Arbor Low, lead mines and battle grounds,
The shivering mountain, Mam Tor and much, much more.

S K Barker

BURTON'S GLORY

A drink at your local, maybe you should
to enjoy Burton's famous brew.
Bass museum a visit so good,
history shared by more than a few.

A horse-drawn heritage tour now you must
save your legs - delight in the show,
the swans gather for their daily crust
and the peaceful River Trent does flow.

A tulip festival in spring for all
at Stapenhill gardens you'll see.
A riverside walk, perhaps play ball
with boat-trips and band music is free.

Burton regatta and riverside show
so much fun for everyone.
Come on, join in now do not be slow
Swell the crowds, look on and see who's won.

Of course shopping precincts for us to roam
free from traffic to pause and browse.
The town hall for functions, not at home
concerts and dances - yes a full house.

Autumn brings the statutes fair to our town
with side-stalls and rides everywhere.
The brewhouse arts centre - wear a gown
entertainment performed with much flair.

There's something for each one of us to find
Burton's glory shines far and wide,
treasures to seek and sports for all kind
pay a call see the sights take a ride.

Margaret Jackson

AUTUMN SOLEMNITY

Somewhere in my singular loss of consciousness
Where autumn's languish droops with weariness upon the city streets
I watched an old wanderer hand over a partially lit cigarette to his friend
The stub quivering amongst fallen embers of gold and brown
'No future for the Railway in Derby' he said

The prodigal yield of this season
Lies swept unfashionably against dark stone walls
Nearby, beneath the vault of heaven St Werberghs Church
Soon to become a shopping arcade, extends a welcome
With hot tea and coffee. But where will they go when
The church entrusted with the interests of its Parish is no more?

Passing from this stolid scene towards the warmth and bright lights indoors
Across the disused weed ridden tracks
Which once like veins pumped the life into the heart of our town
And reverberated to a hundred trains
Only naiveté would fail to recognise our solemnity

D Winson

DERBYSHIRE PRIDE

Tourists come from far and wide
To see the Derbyshire countryside.
The glorious scenery of the Peak
Stately homes and their history seek.
Chatsworth House and park, a prized possession
Breathtakingly beautiful, the first impression.
Historic past and beauty overflow
Which many villages clearly show.
Blue John stone, Halls and Caverns
The Limestone dales, Inns and Taverns.
The quarries which are world renowned
Where the unique Stanton stone is found.

The Derbyshire countryside to the south
Has much scenic beauty where history abounds.
There's the famous Swarkestone Bridge
In the village where I live
Of Bonnie Prince Charlie fame
The bridge to which his *advance guard* came.
Melbourne, a pretty village with much to see
Overflowing with bygone history.
Repton Church with its Saxon Crypt
The school portrayed in the film 'Goodbye Mr Chips'
Derbeians have much to be proud
Embracing Rolls Royce, and the china of Derby Crown.

Betty M Varley

WINNATS PASS

I took a walk down Winnats Pass,
One morning in July.
The sheep were grazing on the grass,
Beneath a cloudless sky.

It was a perfect pastoral scene.
A most idyllic place.
But Winnats grass is not all green,
I know her secret face.

For Winnats on a Winter's day,
Is not the spot to be.
With winds that howl like hounds at bay,
And snowdrifts to your knee.

And weather's not the only thing
That you have got to fear,
For after dark the Banshees sing.
Lives, have been taken here.

One night two travellers I'm told,
A young man and his lass.
Were murdered and found stiff and cold,
Next morn on Winnats Pass.

Some say it is a haunted place,
A pass that should be shun,
And ghostly figures show their face,
After the set of sun.

So go there on a Summer day,
When all is fresh and bright.
Winter's the time to stay away,
And never go at night.

K Ormiston

DERBYSHIRE AS I SEE IT

This *County of Contrasts* I love it so well
From its mountainous peaks to its tiniest dell.
It's not very wide - on the map it stands tall
But it has in its boundaries something for all.
There are rocks, rivers, reservoirs, ruins as well
Much of Derbyshire's history these things can tell.
Many legends, varied customs, the *Well Dressings* are fine
With their floral displays of intriguing design.
Stately homes, famous people, and industry too
Crown China, Blue John Fluorspar, Aero Engines, are a few.
There are sparkling trout streams 'neath the hills and the trees
Some with stepping stones over - beware in the breeze!
Lots of small lively farmsteads with animals galore
And orchards and cornfields, drystone walls and much more.
In the woods, dales and moorlands birds and flowers do abound
Round the hedgerows and ditches much wildlife can be found.
Pretty village, city building, market town, are all here.
That *there'll be nothing to do* you never need fear,
Do you fancy a play, opera, film, or some sport?
Or perhaps there's a craft you would like to be taught.
Take a look at the churches, try their services too
Mosque, Chapel or Temple - Which is God's place for you?
Only two things are missing - the sea and the beach
But though miles away, these are not beyond reach,
Derbyshire's beauty is such though, you'll hardly miss these
As you gaze at the splendour, or wander at ease.
It's a friendly old County, full of interest and hope
Looking onwards and upwards there is no need to mope.
Yes, this County of Derbyshire, I do love it well
But perhaps I am prejudiced, for here I do dwell.

Muriel I Tate

MY DERBYSHIRE MORNING
(Growing up in Ashbourne)

Waking to cock-crow and the cat yawning
breeze brushing the willow-top of my Derbyshire morning.
Spring brought us out like daffodils - flying
down through the Dockey fields, over Ashbourne deep lying.
Grey hills of green Dove-Dale, a crow's flight away
sombrely watched o'er my Derbyshire day.
So I will make a pilgrimage down brook and stream
to the hidden vale where nature flowered in childhood's dream.

Summer was carnival flags in the street,
floats, chaos and colour and dough-nuts to eat.
Park-keeper chased when we ran on the grass
while the one-armed conductor instructed the brass,
golden leaves in the gutter; the sun's last warm rays
at the end of a Summer of Derbyshire days.
So I will make a pilgrimage down brook and stream
to the hidden land where childhood flowered in nature's dream.

The willows in wind will sing me to sleep
with church bells and dog-barks and Derbyshire sheep.
In the dusks of December, safe in bed, tight
protected from spells of the Derbyshire night.
So I will make a pilgrimage down peak and moor
back to the land of innocence on wisdom's shore.
Waking to cock-crow and the cat yawning
breeze brushing the willow-top of my Derbyshire morning.

Peter Dawson

DONKHILL IN JUNE

My bare back teased with breeze
And sunshine, my face looks upward
To the sky. Shadow of a skeleton
Tree dancing in my eye; crooked
Black fingers fragment the blue.
Silent jet pierces the water and
All is still.

Suffocating in silence on velvet
Green, and the bare burnt men are satisfied.
My Father casts, line arcing, settling
Distant as the flies chase around
My face. Jets roar above and skylarks dive
For safety; gone past, and again,
All is still.

Water cracks and breaks, the line pulled;
Shattering the shadow of the skeleton
Tree. My Father mutters, tightening
His grip and the lake bursts
Into the sky, ejecting silver, slithering
Slithering down across the bank and then
All is still.

Joanne Sennitt

GIFT OF LIFE

Three men travelled both day and night
Trying so hard to find that light . . .
A town in the distant so dusty and dry
Bethlehem stood there for all to spy . . .
Lying so snug within a manger
They did find this little stranger . . .
The God above had sent him down
To look after the people of this town . . .
They knelt upon the ground so bare
Throwing their arms up in the air . . .
Upon this day a king was born
On this bleak December morn . . .
Jesus was his name you see
He was sent here for you and me . . .

P Frost

CARSINGTON WATER

I don't think we oughta
Walk round Carsington Water
It's seven and a half miles
And that's not many smiles
When the sky is spitting
And my shoes are ill fitting

Stephen Fell

TWYFORD

A place of serenity,
Water rippling, sunlight through the trees.
Fishermen patiently waiting
For silvery fish and a cool breeze.

Peaceful, birds singing,
Swallows and herons looking for prey.
Sheep in the meadow
Bleating with joy on a summer's day.

Thistles and grasses,
Grassy bank and river wending its way.
Lovely old houses,
A Church, no crowds to keep at bay.

Just nature at its best
Kingfishers, butterflies and blackbird.
A favourite haunt of mine,
Twyford - ssh! Not a word.

Joyce Wakefield

DERBYSHIRE THE HEARTBEAT

Fair shire of the midlands, heartbeat of our sacred isle,
a beauty seldom to be surpassed,
those magical and mystical sites fire the imagination.
Fiery seasonal colours and sceneries attracts artists of all distraction,
whilst passion, peace and tranquillity inspired generations of writers
and poets.
Rolling hills which almost tumble over one another play host to many a
weary walker and rambler,
ancient woodlands and pasture provide safe haven for an abundance of
wildlife,
ferocious rock formations reach out to embrace the clouds, whilst below a
stream of crystal clarity dances fitfully and playfully with nature.
Such a diversity of natural beauty and breathtaking landscapes,
truly our Lord smiled as he blessed the lands where we now proudly prosper.

Michael Hartshorne

TRAVEL WITH ME

Join me in my favourite haunts
places that I go
Matlock with its caves and streams
Mystics we don't know.

Ashbourne with its countryside
a lovely place to be I sit and watch
the silent hills beneath an old
oak tree.
I imagine how at Shrove tide
the people will all cheer I think
I'll come and join them within
the coming year.
It's funny how there's something's
money just can't buy.
Derbyshire so beautiful that
you can't denie.

S H Todd

WHAT IS LOVE?

Love is deep within our hearts
It's the pain one feels when a loved one parts
The bond and strength between best friends
Staying with them until the end
Love is neither thin or fat
No shape has love to be exact
It creeps upon you like winter nights
And is the warmth you feel,
When your lover holds you tight
Love is caring, sharing and giving
But sometimes it's that feeling
You can't go on living
Love is what makes the world go around
You feel like your feet don't touch the ground
Love is in both me and you
Look for love in all you do.

Vanessa E Simpson

A JOURNEY THROUGH DERBYSHIRE

Derbyshire - a county of contrasts galore,
After one visit you'll come back for more,
From Edale to Derby - our city so proud,
Fascinations, discoveries - this shire's endowed.

A tapestry of nature begins with The Peak,
Beautiful dales and walks you may seek,
But if of our history you want to know more,
Museums and libraries - information galore.

It's hard to pick out a favourite place,
The old crooked spire on a church full of grace,
Or, if you wish to see China exquisite,
A trip round Crown Derby's well worth a visit.

As you travel along on a bright summer's day,
There's tradition unique to my shire - a display
Of pictures in flowers - all showered in blessings,
Make sure you don't miss our beloved Well Dressings.

Perhaps stately homes your mind does arouse,
Then your visit has got to include Chatsworth House,
Home of the Duke of Devonshire fine,
Beautiful gardens - flowers smelling like wine.

There's South Wingfield Manor, Haddon Hall and the rest,
Each claiming their own slice of history with zest,
But if on your journey your tummy starts rumbling,
A real Bakewell Pudding will stop all the grumbling.

There's such an assortment of pleasures to mention,
But I've written this tribute with the sole intention,
Of whetting your appetite with a taster or two,
If I have achieved that - then it's over to you . . .

Mary Wheatley

UNTITLED

Where does one start describing beauty that forever stirs the heart
Each new morn awakening to feast our eyes on a new day to start
Hills that meet with water edge be it reservoir lake or stream
Babbling brooks amid pastures lush where one can sit and dream
Pennine and hills covered in dew morning fresh new surprises to view
The majestic sweep of Stonage Edge where breathtaking scenes
around do spread
One feels in awe when taking in the beauty from Downfall of Kinder Scout
The feeling of sheer excitement no words can truly express all one can do
is shout
To look down on a forest of green valleys and streams from a height
that feels serene
Derwent Edge is thrilling indeed when stood by the towering Salt Cellar
how insignificant we seem
Wolfscote Dale with its stone amid grass sweeping hills within quiet
hours to pass
Wonderful Goyt Valley variety to suit all tastes spoilt for choice of
route to choose or inviting trail to take
The soft quiet appeal of Dove Dale rustic bridges taking one to winding
paths of adventure where silence itself can be heard
Broken only by lovely sounds of creatures most of which are birds
Torrs Park where the meeting of two rivers Sett and Goyt whose water
below New Mills do flow.
So much to encounter to feel to taste lifting the spirits giving the heart a glow
Ruins and sites of a bygone age where life centred around a village green
Children laughing around a may-pole did play and life more simple
must have been.

W Kuczaj

HEAVEN'S GATE (AN ODE TO DERBYSHIRE)

Derbyshire is more beautiful than words can say, people so friendly,
She is a foretaste of heaven, clearly God's county,
If you wish to take a dynamic trip back into history
Experience the Blue-John mines near Castleton
And the plague village of Eyam, not forgetting God's natural beauty,
Or thirteenth century Ashbourne Church of St. Oswald
Being shaped internally like Christ's cross on Calvary,
Medieval shops and streets - a rare treat,
Spending time relieved of burden and care
Deeply enriches the quality of life, imagination and spirit free,
I am very privileged daily warming my heart, I dare be bold
To boast 0 Derbyshire infiltrates with contentment, feeding spiritually.

Having travelled as far as Iona and Torquay in Devon
I feel Derbyshire, in gorgeous variety, is a vision of heaven,
Apart from Army service in Kent my years of thirty seven
Have been spent in an intense love affair with this divine Shire county
Of Derby. A joyful time spent as tour guide for the young
At Derby Cathedral - a mammoth bounty,
Wherein lies the monument to four times married Bess of Hardwick -
                                                    such a feature,
Trusting no-one so built it before death being a vain creature,
You may recall her when naming her houses I guess,
There were four - including Hardwick Hall and original Chatsworth House,
A wealth of treasure lies behind the Cathedral door and more,
To experience in God's house, by the altar over there
We have recreated the appearance of the Holy dove
With peace, fellowship, and prayerful Christian love.

Derbyshire contains picturesque villages, farms, country walks by the score
Not forgetting Chesterfield's Crooked Spire, market - and more
Within this young Diocese - born in nineteen twenty seven,
Of the many places I have travelled to or seen
Derbyshire is the fairest, radiant, Queen,
Come to experience yourself the joys of earthly heaven.

Kevin E Sims

82

DERBYSHIRE DELIGHTS

If you are searching for the sea . . . it isn't here!
No sandy beach, or stony cove . . . *For this is Derbyshire.*

You will find the Derwent, Dove and Wye . . . gentle rivers flowing.
On the banks, wild flowers . . . and wild garlic growing
Where once Isaac Walton, the famous angler came,
His book inspired all fishermen, which enhanced his fame.

A landscape of such diversity . . . gorges, valleys deep,
Streams meander thro' green pastures dotted with grazing sheep.
Rocky outcrops, dark forests; peaceful dales . . . idyllic.
Nestling into hillsides bleak farms of tile and brick.
Scattered villages, cottages built with local stone
Gardens bright with flowers, there drowsy bees drone.
In the High Peak the stark beauty of limestone walls
Are seen. On lonely moors, the curlew calls.
Red Shanks and Grouse are heard and rare Golden Plover.
Surprises in plenty, more delights to discover.

I will walk the Pennine Way. Find magic mystic places,
Caverns, damp caves, strange shapes of rock faces.
The Blue John mine . . . 'fluorspar' . . . world wide is known
Crafted into ob-jet d'art, and jewellery from this stone.
I will visit Country Estates, romantic medieval castles
Reversing time . . . in mind . . . to legends and historic battles.
Recalling the lovers who fled over the bridge at Haddon,
From that fateful day, was known as 'Dorothy Vernon'.
Traditions survived through the years to modern times.
Treasures to cherish, a hope to preserve pastimes.
Taste the Ashbourne gingerbread, sample Bakewell Tart.
Enjoy this County you have seen, take it to your heart.

If you are searching for the sea . . . it isn't here!
No sandy beach, or stony cove . . . *For This Is Derbyshire.*

J Newstead

TRENT VALLEY

Here where juggernauts rumble south the legions strode
Heading for Litocetum down the Ryknild Way,
Broke for breakfast where the Happy Eater stands
Or camped where the village Co-op sits,
Leaving a dividend of lost denarii.

Here where the lonely fisherman casts his fly and swans parade
Questing Danes, pushing from Repton up the swollen Trent,
Grounded and, liking the promise of the virgin land,
Built their rough dwellings on the nearest knoll,
Leaving behind their name of Tucklesholme.

Here where the pleasure boat waits at the weeping lock
Sweating and cursing navvies dug the cut.
Great horses, snorting in the frosty air,
Hauled garish barges burdened with bricks or beer,
Leaving small waterfowl and bankside pub.

Here where sleek-nosed streamers link city to city
Platemen laboured for monsters of steam and steel,
Breaking the clamorous night with racing fire,
To feed deep appetites of mill and forge,
Leaving a lance struck through the valley's heart.

Now in this autumn half-light here from my window's eye,
Under the eerie glow of the sodium lamps,
Gangers and bargees labour in shadowed silence,
Red-haired Danes ravage sly in the dusk,
A ghostly centurion urges marching men.

Neil Adams

DIALECT DELIGHTS

My Uncle John,
Although he has gone
To a land across the sea,
Remembers dear Derby when he cries:
'Hey up, me duck', or 'Well bugger me!'

Lisa Ollerenshaw

THE PLACE TO BE

Stately homes and gardens, rivers running by
Sleepy village, distant all pleasing to the eye.

Then in contrast, industry, smoke and fumes abound.
Opencast mineworkers, tearing up the ground.

Lovely churches, lively towns, busy markets too.
Hills, dales and craggy cliffs are there to welcome you.

Where is this little Eden? Go on, ask, enquire,
You'll soon find out, it's all around in lovely Derbyshire.

Elsie Cresswell

THE PEAK DISTRICT

I looked deep into the valley and there I saw a vortex of wind
bullying the crispy, bronze coloured leaves as it picked them
up and tossed them from side to side.

The trees that once stood so proud seem to stretch out for
mercy as if they were being humiliated and stripped to a
nakedness of defeat.

The birds that live in the valley where food was once plentiful,
now seek refuge in the gardens of mankind where they can
pillage for food which is left out openly.

Yet they seek revenge for the waters that have frozen and
beg no mercy for the milk they steal to quench their dying
thirst.

The squirrels that live high in the trees are buried deep in
their drays with enough food to smother them. But they know
they will need all the nuts and acorns to survive because of
the bleak conditions nature has bestowed upon them.

The flowers that once swayed gently in the summer breeze are
now slowly being suffocated by the gripping frost and their
fragile backs are being crushed into the ground by the ice and
falling snow. As they die they know it is not in vain,
because the seeds they once planted in this fertile ground will
bestow them back their honour in the beauty of their children
yet to come.

Spring is on its way now, the buds and young saplings stretch and
yawn to see the delights of the sun. Even the trees don't feel
so naked now because their leaves have started to come.

Christopher Newton

GLOSSOP A TWIN? (NAHH)

Now, I'll tell you a story, about Glossop Town.
It's the most beautiful place, for miles around.
'Gateway to the Peaks' as it's sometimes known.
With its heather covered hills, where I often roam.
They say we 'ave a twin town called Bad-Villbel or sommat.
Now that statement fair bring a pain t' my stomach.
You can forget them places, in Germany an' France.
They 'ave no open moorland like th' Glossop expanse.
You can walk by th' banks of a bubblin' stream.
Or stroll through th' 'eather, content with your dream.
To follow th' path a Roman legion took,
Is much better than reading it in a stuffy old book.
It's a very old place, where history abounds.
You'll not find a likeness in a European town.
Glossop was, once, a town famous for cotton.
But th' mills 'ave, long since closed, an' all but forgotten.
There's two lovely parks, full of trees an' flowers,
That wer' bequeathed to us by th' noble Lord Howard.
You'll never find its likeness, in Europe or anywhere.
Glossop is singular, never one of a pair.

Michael A Greaves

DERBYSHIRE

The hills and dales of Derbyshire
bring comfort and relief
From snow and hail and rainstorms
Invading our world, like a thief.

The warm stone walls give shelter,
For sheep and cows to seek,
Trees cast their leaves and warm the ground
Where hedgehogs lie asleep!

The Derbyshire spring is splendid
When all of life unfurls
From lime green buds, to cellandines
And the hedgehog now uncurls!

In summertime, the meadow
is full of rich, green grass,
The woods alight in full bloom now
with wild flowers amass.

The rivers, hills and valleys
in autumn time, now glow
With gold and red and orange,
before the winter snow.

Snow caps the hills in winter,
Ice coats reservoirs in a shell,
Frost turns branches into crystal
And, Derbyshire's beauty casts its spell.

Shirley Williamson

THE DERBYSHIRE COUNTRYSIDE

Oh Derbyshire, oh Derbyshire, I long to be with you,
To just spot instantaneously that perfect English view!
To stroll around the peaks and dales to see what I can see,
And feel the pleasure in my bones like someone who is free!
As I gaze on those grassy hills to view the lovely sight,
My heart breaks out into a dance like moonbeams in the night!
And so I say if you are bored and want somewhere to go,
Just make your way to Derbyshire: I'm sure you'll love it so!

Sharon Howells

LIFE IN THE DALES

The church, with the,
Crooked Spire,
Stands regal,
And grand, surrounded,
By parishioners, and
Shoppers, with money,
In hand.

The hills all round,
With the golf pitches,
And sounds of cattle,
And farmers, tending,
The lands.

Birds fly high,
Landing on trees,
The hills of the Peak,
Are ready to climb,
One by one children,
And all kind.

Horses tramp through the,
Woods and fields,
Riders, content to,
Take in the view,
Of the hills,
Where wild flowers,
Grow in grass fields,
So much beauty,
For all to behold.

Barbara Brown

HOMELANDS

Be bold, cry, leap,
Sing for the country which lives in you.
Not for society
Or the system by what we must live.
But for the land,
For the soul of the earth.
In those who seek only to be free
Justice is too heavy a burden.
Uplift your soul in the knowledge
That the earth on which one walks seeks harmony,
But retain; those who walk crave power.
Be liberated in thought
And no man may claim
This beautiful, orange, free land.

Y R Walker

DERBY - DERBYSHIRE

Wide open countryside
Tight terraced streets
Canals that meander
Rivers to meet

Factory chimneys
Smoke clouds billowing
Hillside cottages
Graceful trees willowing

Makers of engines
Locomotive and Aero
Fine bone china
Old patterned and neo

Historical houses
Bursting with treasure
Thundering theme parks
Providing our leisure

Quiet cold churches
Noisy hot discos
Peaks packed with hikers
Back-packs and thermos

A footballing city
'The rams' - what a team
And cricket is played here
White flannels on green

So this is my county
My city my home
So proud to be native
Ne'er far will I roam.

Erica J Bellini

FLAMES OF LOVE

As Milly stared into reddened fire,
Her dreams began to aspire.
For when Milly was young a toiled day at her local farm,
Was like a raging storm before the calm.
She had little time for affection or love,
Her husband was killed in the great war spare a prayer for Milly
                                        heavens above
Daily routine was the same seven days a week every year,
Even Christmas was spent working at the farm with falling tear.
As the years went by the children grew strong and times got better,
Weaker Milly grew like the day she received that deathly letter.
That letter which gave her heartache when she knew her mate had died,
Only forward she could look the best she as tried.
The children have gone now married some to the East some to the West,
Like birds they have flown in life to build their own nest.
As Milly draws the old armchair closer to the dancing flames,
She sees the ones she loves and the loss no one she blames.
For she has found the answer to her darkest nightmare,
Heaven she has found into flames of love she forever gives a stare.

John Watson

94

DERBYSHIRE

As I roam the hills of Derbyshire
There is peace within my soul
Not for me the bustle of cities
Nor the walkways of life
Unfolding beneath the
Water's flowing bowl

But to walk hand in hand
With the spirit of love
And kindness
And to carry the burden
Of helping others as
They find joy and peace
Roaming those self same
Hills
Then I will have achieved
My goal.

P Holmes

WOMAN OF ART

She talks amongst a group of friends,
Slowly sipping a glass of wine,
Her eyes sparkle with passion,
Her lips are tender pink,
Like the purest snow,
She makes me feel excited again,
She teases without knowing,
Legs crossed, her dress reveals
Tanned legs showing.

Sexuality, curves of beauty,
Perfection that could destroy a man,
Her features sparkle more than diamonds
Or the summer sun.
I love her more than I think to please,
Her aura leaves me weak and drained,
Like a moth seduced by a flickering flame,
I ache inside, with a lusting heart,
To touch and be near this woman of art.

Philip May

ALZHEIMER'S DISEASE

Watching you trying to sort out in your mind
Who you are, who we are.
All your loved ones always around.
Watching the pain in mum's eyes.
Wishing you could have been together at home,
For the rest of your days.
But she never complains,
For she will be there for you, always.

Alison Rainsford

A WOODS LAMENT

O woods called Weekly hall where are you now?
We watched the woodsmen plunder every living bough
Where primrose danced around trees mossy feet
And bluebells misty drift is now deplete
So many happy hours, in spring was spent
among the dark, deep rutted ridings, which meant
So much to children born in town's confines
To breath untainted air and smell the scented vines;
In summer just to walk within your shade
And picnic feast in one of your cool glades
Living for a brief and wondrous time
as Robin Hood, committing his imaginary crimes,
Or other legendary heroes we'd pretend
Until our day of fantasy would end,
Autumn, as the yellowing leaves would flutter down
And the fresh green cloak of summer changed to brown
For nuts, we would with squirrels now compete
In search of chestnut, beech and hazel round our feet
Gathered among the crispy dying spread
of leaves, as nature makes her winter bed;
Where once I heard the thrush and linnet sing
Now the thud of dynamite in my ears ring
As this haven that we thought was ours for keeps
Was raised down to the ground as quarry creeps
along to gouge out seams of ironstone,
Leaving fields of clay, so stark and so alone;
Now as across the landscape I peruse
I picture in my mind the long gone views
of trees majestic, reining grand,
Part of the forest that once covered all this land
Pray that some wooded havens we will spare
For our children, the countryside to share
To know the pleasures that we knew
But Weekly hall woods, we're sorry, for we grieve too
late for you.

David A Garrett

NORTHAMPTONSHIRE

Northamptonshire the rose of the shires
This poem it inspires
Its pleasant greenery
Serenity of the scenery
See it all boy oh boy
Pleasure it gives and boundless joy

From Pytchley comes the hunt
Beagles, horses, horns as well
Huntsmen in colourful attire
They look swell
Watch as they ride
So colourful in the countryside

Wicksteed's park in all its glory
People travel far and wide
To have a swing and a slide
On the train for a joyful ride

Around the lakeside
It fills the children with glee
Surely a feature for all to see

Kettering's parish church with its spire so tall
Towering over the market stalls
Beckoning, calling, to one and all
I am a Northamptonshire person
I love it all

B W Jones

ALWAYS A RAINBOW

Van Gogh? No, a field of rape,
and next to that the poppies blaze,
to dazzle, and defy our eyes
not to gaze, and gaze, and gaze.

Hedges of May, and Queen Anne's Lace,
with honeysuckle tumbling down,
and smoky, smouldering old man's beard,
far from the glass, and bricks of town.

Pink horse-chestnut spires, green limes,
golden cattle, rooks building high:
river meandering through the valley,
a sombre grey, neath a blue-dappled sky.

Purple the blackberries, scarlet the hips,
and as seasons come, and as seasons go,
there's always a rainbow in Northamptonshire,
but if you live here, of course you know.

Kathleen Pateman

NOTTINGHAM GOOSE FAIR

Can you hear the music of the fair
Can you smell the evening air
All the noises and the smells
Especially all of the bells
Ringing and dinging
Toffee apples for sale
Including ale
The roller coaster
What a boaster
On the dodgems people shout
Let's go on the round-a-bout
Fish and chips
And apple pips
Sausages and sauce
Oh come and buy some
Let's have a look at the horse
It's getting late, time to go home
So in the car you get
I'm going to bed
Hooray for Nottingham Goose Fair.

Mary Skelton

MY NOTTINGHAM

Nottingham oh Nottingham
City of our birth!
With castle bold
And churches old
Greens windmill,
Robin Hood.
Your lovely lace
And full of grace
The arc of Colwick Wood.
Buses green
Enhance the scene,
Mixed nations
Share abodes
Traffic rumbles
Into town
And mingles on the roads.
Council house
Market square
Pigeons by the droves.

Twice weekly
Sneinton market
Is held in open air,
For centuries
The marketers
Have stood
And bartered there.
Hurrah Goose Fair!
With brandy snaps
Sweet candy floss
As well -
Let's ride the horses
Slide the slide
How lovely
Hot dogs smell!

On Saturdays -
'Come on you Reds'
'Come on you Magpies' too
The chant and cheers
Of lads and girls
Is really nothing new.
The winding Trent
Flows swiftly on
We know not where
Nor why
Nottingham oh Nottingham
To you we say goodbye.

Shirley Aplin

SHORT CHANGE

'The change will do you good'. She said,
As she looked me in the eye.
'You know you've had a nasty chest',
'Although I can't think why'.

'The change will do you good'. She said,
As she opened up my case.
'Aunt Edith will be pleased you know',
'To see your dead white face'.

'The change will do you good'. She said,
As she packed my woolly vest.
'I know she'll make your stay worth while',
'Her cooking is the best'.

'I know the change will do you good',
'You'll enjoy it every day'.
'Aunt Edith with her jokes and things',
'Enjoyment every way'.

I couldn't stand this ancient crone,
And her burnt old cooking range.
No tele' and the bone hard beds,
Still, perhaps there's been a change.

A B Hughes

ENOUGH IS ENOUGH

She never actually believed,
That he would leave,
His woman, his home, his bed,
But his heart just missed,
That fateful beat,
And I don't love you is all
That he said.

He packed up his things
In an old suitcase,
His clothes, his photos, his love,
Never stopping once for a moment
To think,
Just repeating enough is enough.

She watched him walk,
And she couldn't talk,
She sat, she laughed, she cried,
She just couldn't understand,
Why her life was such a mess,
And why his love had died . . .

Marie Harmer

AN UNTITLED VERSE OF AN OLD AGE PENSIONER

Weary is a heart which can not love it gets wearier still
As days go by.
Weary is a life which poses the question why don't I
Just die.
For life to me is a weary old place,
It brings me down without much grace,
As I look at myself in the mirror and cannot
Recognise my face,
For I have changed and grown old,
And can count happy memories on one hand so
Cold,
So white so wrinkled and so bony,
Why is it now I feel so lonely?
As life seems to have passed me by
And for that I can not cry,
As I observe life going on around me so strong,
But feel no part of it for in this generation I don't
Belong.

Emma Kemm

THE WELCOME CITY

Nottingham is my home town,
It's always the top never down,
There's the castle and Wollaton Park,
And Little John the clock lit up when dark,
Plus the council house in slab square
We also boast the famous Goose Fair,
Robin Hood and the Boxer Bendigo,
William Booth and Salvation Army you all know,
Victoria Centre and Broad Marsh with shops galore,
But the famous Drury Hill is no more,
Theatre Royal with plays for pleasure,
Our coat of arms 'A jewel a real treasure',
Nottingham famous world wide for the best lace,
We boast the prettiest girls they are ace,
Arboretum, pond and lovely flower show,
For Sherwood Forest you've not far to go,
Queen's Medical Centre Prince Charles did treat,
Our Sheriff of Nottingham no one can beat,
Jessie Boot the university did give,
A campus with a lake, where students live,
Palace De Dance the ballroom, a first,
The trip to Jerusalem to quench your thirst,
A city centre beach with real sand,
St Peter's church a real gem so grand,
Just a few of our landmarks more than some,
So to this great city you all must come,
England, Scotland and Wales nice places to test,
But I tell you Nottingham is the best,
Just to finish Radio Nottingham tune in
New 96.2 Trent FM with money you can win
So do come try your luck
Just a bit of slang 'It's lovely mi duck'.

Clem

BURTON JOYCE. NOTTS.

A lovely little village, sits alongside the River Trent,
Where in fine and clement weather, many happy hours are spent,
It has some lovely little winding lanes, and is also very clean,
Has many lovely evergreens, and stately trees complete the scene.

Some picturesque little cottages, many painted black and white,
With roses growing round the door, a truly lovely sight,
Four churches also stand so proud, to welcome all into the fold,
An awe inspiring sight indeed, so exciting to behold.

A very small railway station, set next to the fields and wild life,
Some lovely quaint old pubs, where you can take your family and
your wife.
The children are not forgotten, they can play where you can see,
And catering is truly good, and if not wanting alcohol so is the coffee
and the tea.

Yet this quiet little village, has a full and vigorous life,
Much charity work is done, by both husband and by wife,
They are a very caring community, help each-other very much,
And though they may be out of town, are never out of touch.

Eileen Handley

OLD HOUSE

The house that once stood proud and tall
Now faces demolition
Brick by old grey brick she'll fall
beyond all recognition

Forming clouds of dust and mortar
When they begin the dreadful slaughter
Crashing and tumbling to the ground
Making such an eerie sound

'Remember my past years' she'll call
Creaking and groaning from wall to wall
Old house, proud house
What secrets you must know
Old house, proud house
I'm grieved to see you go
Yielding to the hands of time
I wish old house, that you'd been mine

Liz Young

DON'T LOOK BACK

I'd recently retired at the age of sixty five,
So now I'd time to stop and think, it's good to be alive,
I thought I'll go to Leicester, and wander round the town,
To see what they are putting up, and what they're pulling down
I walked along the High Street, and had to stop and stare,
The well remembered shops had gone, and Union St not there,
The Clock Tower I was glad to see, still standing straight and tall,
But all the litter flying round, I didn't like at all,
The Leicester I remembered was clean with streets well swept,
The one I found was dirty, not much of it was left.
Bond St which I finally found after quite a lot of trouble
Gave me quite a shock, for it was just a pile of rubble,
The Bell Hotel I used to love for Saturday Evening 'Hops'
Was gone, and in its place, a maze of corridors and shops,
I walked back to the Station, my feelings grim and black,
If that's the best that they can do, I won't be going back . . .

C Chapman

LEICESTER CITY

Now let us see what we have here,
A city of interest that's very clear,
The ever popular De Montford Hall,
Where you can see a concert or have a ball,
The Museum and the famous New Walk
Where you can wander or sit and talk.
You make a date, you want to meet but where,
Where else of course but the Town Hall square,
The Caribbean Carnival a feature of the year
It's colourful, cheerful and always full of cheer.
There's many famous people that we mustn't overlook
Simon de Montford, Cardinal Wolsely and Thomas Cook
Richard and David Attenborough, Humperdink, Jo Orton
That wrote many a famous book.
Just look closely in every nook and cranny
Places of interest I'm sure you'll find many
Leicester is really a historical place.
Truly full of interest, charm and grace.

Eileen Neal

A SILENT SADNESS

I went for a walk in Bradgate Park today,
And as I strolled along the way
I could see hills of bracken and fallow deer
Peahens and rabbits began to appear.
The mansion ruins are still to be seen
Which was the birthplace of Lady Jane Grey
our ill-fated nine days queen.
Lady Jane a popular young lady, from stories told.
Who was executed when she was only sixteen years old.
On hearing the news about Jane the Bradgate Park
woodcutters anger reared,
They chopped the tops off the 'Pollard Oakes'
as their tears appeared.
These mighty oakes which stand tall and proud,
Mark a time in history when Lady Jane lay in a shroud.
An untimely death which seems to be madness
For one so young I feel a silent sadness
The trees are a reminder of this young nine days queen.
Even to this day the 'Pollard Oakes' are still to be seen.

Margaret Betts

A ROSE BY ANY OTHER

The War of the Roses:
A struggle for power in a distant past,
commemorated now by flags and buildings;
surrounded by the irony of nature's peace.

It is hard to imagine the carnage;
The hurt.
The blood.
The death.

Billboards speak of the glory of victory
and few think of those who suffered.

A single rock marks the spot
where Richard Plantagenet stood.
A crystal-white rose placed at its base
acts as a memorial to the slain.

'A horse, a horse, my kingdom for a horse',
The Christ-like plea echoes across the battlefield.
I hear the gallop of hooves on Ambion's slope,
The clash of metal upon metal.

My somber thoughts disturb me,
I contemplate the lessons learnt that day,
as the Last Post resounds
across October's dull and dusky skyline.

Mike Brown

LEICESTERSHIRE

Home of my birth, and childhood dreams,
    Leafy winding lanes and rippling streams.
Bright meadows of buttercups and clover,
    Where as children we loved to play.
Why could we not stay all day?

Fields of cows and horses grazing,
    The scent of new mown hay,
The small tea-house, where we called on our way.

Picnics by the river,
    Watching the swans glide by,
A moment of tranquillity
    Under a clear blue sky.

Quaint country pubs, so warm and gay,
    A welcoming rest, at the end of the day.
Country cottages and stately homes,
    This is the Leicestershire, I love to roam.

Birdsong at eventide,
    As I walk the woodland paths.
Find an echo in my heart,
    Of those days, long since past.

Seasons come and go,
    Each with a beauty all their own.
But the timeless charm of Leicestershire,
    Will always be my home.

Margaret J Robinson

TO VISITORS

Leicester is known for many a thing
like De Montfort Hall where the famous sing.
Haymarket Theatre for drama and art
The Little and *Pheonix* stage their part.
The sporting fanatics do well of course
with Rugby, Cricket and maybe a Horse.
Football at Filbert we watch our Blues
back page of The Mercury making the news.
History surrounds this midlands shire
So much to see you couldn't possibly tire.
From Lady Jane to ghost of Guild Hall
New Walk museum and Jewry Wall.
The Magazine bloody tales do tell
from who took part, to when, and who fell.
Beautiful countryside for us to see
different every season, aren't we lucky.

Helen Tedder

THE HARVEST FESTIVAL

It's time for the Harvest
Fruitful and mellow
Ripe rosie apples and corn so yellow
Bread that's made from the flour
that's ground.
Smiling faces all around.

Children singing in the Sunday
School choir.
All dressed up in their
Sunday attire.
God bless the seasons one
and all
Spring summer autumn and
winter's call.

J S Burton

THE BATTLE FOR LEICESTER

The shire of Leicester has seen many battles.
Ghosts howl their tales in the wind,
Mixing stories of which are the most noble.
Silence covers the one considered inane,
Although its battle ground today is clearly marked.

With colours held high,
And a mighty roar,
Both sides clashed as equals.

But soon came the screams.
Foul wind carried its horrors.
The level field became a mountain.
Spirits were sipped until hollow.
Hearts dripped dry.

With battle lost.
Its field no longer lights the sky.
Their standard lowered.

No more Premiership football for Leicester.

Dewi Wyn Hughes

THE WIND

The trees swayed and swished slowly and soundly,
The leaves began to race and the humans quickened their pace.
The wind rushed forwards, twisting and twirling,
Forever swirling.
It tiptoed behind a man and pounced suddenly on his back,
The man's muscles flexed and reflexed,
H is bones shivered and clattered.
The wind picked up its speed and dived into the air,
Hurrying,
And scurrying,
Not worrying what damage it could do.
It plunged into the trees, wrapping itself around them.
The leaves sailed into the air pirouting.
Branches struggled to keep hold.
Still tugging the wind revolved around the trees,
Coiling, twirling, curling and whirling.
The branches broke off, they could strive no longer,
The trees rushed down in a shamble.
The wind loved prancing about,
So it dashed into a house,
And made the windows wobble and clutter.
It made babies cry,
Children cold.
It even swooped into the sea,
Making it swish and sway,
Also making the waves crash loudly together.
The wind pressed on and zoomed up into the sky.
It looked for something it could pluck,
But grew tired,
So it wandered off and went in a wend, dispersing.

Kathryn Ferguson

HEROES ALL

To arms, to arms, war has begun
Loud throbs the echo of a once silent drum
A bugler sounds his last note
With his life blood spattering his coat.
Up to their knees in mud
Begrimed with dirt and sodden with blood
For their countries call, they were heroes all.
Out of the night comes a warrior's battle cry
They stumble and fall and heroes die.
In the grey mist of the morning light
The relief party beheld this sight
With bowed heads and clasped hands they,
Prayed their comrades be delivered to better lands
The captain looked as the glory fell dead
With hand on sword he slowly said
For their countries call they were heroes all.

C Taperell

INFORMATION

We hope you have enjoyed reading this book - and th at you will continue to enjoy it in the coming years.

If you like reading and writing poetry drop us a line, or give us a call, and we'll send you a free information pack.

Write to

Anchor Books Information
1-2 Wainman Road
Woodston
Peterborough
PE2 7BU.